# A TASTE OF HOSPITALITY:
*Authentic Ghanaian Cookery*

Marian Shardow MHCIMA

Printed in Victoria, Canada

**National Library of Canada Cataloguing in Publication**

Shardow, Marian
 A taste of hospitality / Marian Shardow.
 ISBN 1-55395-218-9
 1. Cookery, Ghanaian.    I. Title.
TX725.G4S46 2002        641.59667            C2002-904913-X

# TRAFFORD

**This book was published *on-demand* in cooperation with Trafford Publishing.**
On-demand publishing is a unique process and service of making a book available for retail sale to the public taking advantage of on-demand manufacturing and Internet marketing.
**On-demand publishing** includes promotions, retail sales, manufacturing, order fulfilment, accounting and collecting royalties on behalf of the author.

2404 Government St., Victoria, B.C. V8T 4L7, CANADA
Phone        250-383-6864        Toll-free    1-888-232-4444 (Canada & US)
Fax          250-383-6804        E-mail       sales@trafford.com
Web site     www.trafford.com   TRAFFORD PUBLISHING IS A DIVISION OF TRAFFORD HOLDINGS LTD.
Trafford Catalogue #02-0932        www.trafford.com/robots/02-0932.html

10        9        8        7        6        5        4        3        2        1

# A TASTE OF HOSPITALITY:
*Authentic Ghanaian Cookery*

## About The Author

On the 6 June 1957, the Shardow family was blessed with a precious beautiful baby girl, a joy to her family, Marian Shardow. An encourager and a pillar of strength to many.

She is the oldest of five children. Her dad promised her something no one could take from her (knowledge) in order for her to soar to the height of her possibilities, so he sent her to the Achimota school in Ghana, a school renowned for bringing up leaders. After her secondary education she came to England to further her education. She studied at Westminster College, Vincent Square, London SW1, renowned for being the best hotel school. Marian gained a Diploma in Hotel and Catering studies. She went on to study for the Final Membership of the Hotel, Catering & International Management Association.

Her career to date has been centred specifically but not exclusively on Residential Management. She worked as a Technical Instructor training people with mental health problems and learning disabilities in catering and other skills.

Presently, she works at Imperial College as a Hall Manager at Southside Halls. She is a woman with many talents, innovative and good interpersonal skills. Her interests are far and wide but most of all she enjoys Christian fellowship, going to the theatre, swimming, music and last but not least cooking. This is a woman who will bring inspiration to all.

# Introduction

This is a book of cooking everyday at any time of the year. Meals for all occasions.

I hope it will give you both pleasure and inspiration.

I would like to express my thanks to the team at Print Inc., Ability, Renfrew Road, for putting the contents of this book together for me. Well done! Thanks to Uncle Ben and Auntie Sheila for the encouragement and support they gave to me.

The Ghanaian hospitality reflects the kingdom of heaven. *Rom 12:13*. Our culture is based on the Bible. We see food as a therapy. The way to one's heart is through the stomach. We share fellowship through eating. Our culture teaches us the gift of sharing. Our hospitality brings us the miracles.

We are generous and we share our food with the poor, so we are a blessed people. *Proverbs 22*.

This book is an offering unto the Lord for the wonderful skills he has given me. I thank God for the inspiration he gives me to bless people with my cooking. Through this many have come to Christ.

It is also dedicated to the Woman of Noble Character in *Proverbs 31–10:20*.

Hospitality is a blossoming of love in our homes where love is tended all the year through.

The welcome, the friendship shared, the drinks offered (even if it is a mere glass of cold water) and the meals cooked, however simple, are ways of expressing love to all who come in.

For the country where hospitality blossoms is one where love has a permanent place. Better to eat vegetables with people you love than to eat the finest meat where there is hate. *Proverbs 15*.

The people of Ghana have warm hearts. I thank God for Ghanaians.

For whatever crisis or trouble people live through, everyone has to eat. The birth of a child, a bereavement or someone in the

7

family in hospital, all mean there is less time for the day to day run - ning of the home. So to call briefly with something ready to eat is a really practical way of showing them how much we care about them and an opportunity to share our gift of hospitality which certainly spreads the love of God.

Through the routine chores of washing, cooking and cleaning with love and the help of God we make happy memories.

This book is dedicated in gratitude to God Almighty and to my father Zubeiro Baba Shardow, a former Member of Parliament and the National Organiser of the Ghana Young Pioneer Movement under the late Dr Kwame Nkrumah, to whom I owe all that I have become and more than I can repay.

'Daddy, I salute you.'

And to my dear Mum, Beatrice, you are the queen of my heart. Sweet mother, how could I forget you?

*Soups*

# FISHERMAN'S SOUP (NSASWIA)

*1 kilo fresh fish*
*1 fish stock cube*
*1.75 litres of water*
*4 spring onions*
*1 teaspoon fresh ground ginger*
*1 tin plum tomatoes (240 gms)*
*pepper to taste (chilli)*
*1 clove garlic (crushed)*
*salt*
*1 onion*

*Serves 2*

Clean and cut the fish into pieces and put into a saucepan with the fish stock, ginger, garlic, salt and water. Chop and add the onions. Place the saucepan on the fire and simmer until the onions are soft. Blend the tomatoes and chillies, then add to the soup. Cook gently for 30 mins, then add the chopped spring onions. Serve hot with Fufu or Banku or potatoes.

# OKRA SOUP (OKRO)

*10 okras (lady fingers)*
*500 gms mutton*
*1 tablespoon smoked prawns or shrimps*
*500 gms smoked or fresh fish*
*2.75 litres water*
*1 onion*
*pepper (chilli)*
*125 gms mushrooms*
*3 garden eggs or 1 medium aubergine*
*3 large fresh tomatoes*
*or 1 small tin plum tomatoes (400 gms)*
*1 teaspoon crushed fresh ginger*
*1 chicken stock cube*
*salt to taste*

*Serves 6*

Wash and cut the mutton into pieces and put into a saucepan with the chopped onions, stock cube and salt. Place on the fire for 5 mins stirring occasionally. Add the water and cook for 10 mins. Wash the okras, garden eggs or peeled aubergine and chillies and add to the stock. Cook until the vegetables are tender. Remove the vegetables from the soup. Wash the mushrooms, shrimps or prawns and the fish and add to the soup. Blend the tomatoes, chillies and garden eggs with a little water. Return to the saucepan. Mash the okras. Return to the saucepan. Cook the soup gently for 30 mins. Serve with fufu or banku.

For vegetarians please omit the mutton, fish and shrimps or prawns. Add carrots and sweet red pepper.

# SPINACH SOUP (BAA WONU)

*8 mushrooms*
*500 gms smoked game or fish*
*1 large onion*
*1 tin plum tomatoes (400 gms)*
*6 young nkontomire leaves (kalaloo) or 250 gms frozen spinach*
*1 vegetable stock cube*
*salt to taste*
*chillies to taste*
*2.5 litres water*

*Serves 6*

Wash the green leaves in salt water, if bought fresh, and boil. Wash and cut the game or fish into pieces. Put into a saucepan with the chopped onions, chillies, salt and water. Place on the stove. Wash and add the mushrooms. Blend the plum tomatoes and add to the soup. Remove the chillies when tender and blend, then return to the soup. Add the stock cube. Blend the cooked green leaves and add to the soup. If using frozen spinach add to the soup at this stage. Cook gently for 30 mins. Serve hot with fufu.

# DRIED BEAN SOUP

*100 gms dried broad beans*
*500 gms mutton*
*250 gms smoked fish*
*1 tin plum tomatoes (400 gms)*
*3 garden eggs or 1 medium aubergine*
*salt and chillies to taste*
*1 large onion*
*2.25 litres water*
*1 Maggi cube*

*Serves 6*

Soak the broad beans overnight in water. Wash and put into a saucepan. Add the water and cook until tender. Wash and cut the mutton into pieces and put into a saucepan. Add a little water and the chopped onions and place on the stove. Add the chillies and cook until tender. Blend the tomatoes, pepper and beans and add to the soup. Add a Maggi cube. Add the rest of the water. Add the fish and season to taste. Let it simmer for about 45 mins. Serve hot with plantain fufu.

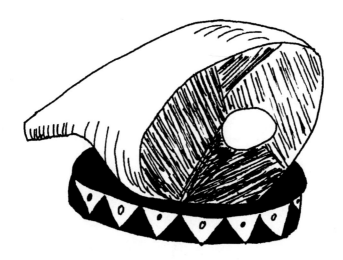

# Millet Soup

*1 medium onion*
*½ cup powdered fish*
*½ cup millet flour*
*1 teaspoon all purpose seasoning*
*3 cups water*
*1 small tin plum tomatoes (240 gms)*

*Serves 2*

Put the water on the stove to boil. Add the all purpose seasoning and the powdered fish. Blend the tomatoes and add to the soup. Add the millet flour and stir. Simmer for 30 mins. Serve with banku, fufu or tuo.

# PITO YEAST SOUP

*100 gms pito yeast*
*1 small tin plum tomatoes (240 gms)*
*½ kilo mutton or fish*
*season all*
*1 medium onion*
*1 litre water*
*chillies to taste*

*Serves 4*

Wash and cut the mutton or fish into pieces. Put into a saucepan and put on the stove for 5 mins to seal in the juices. Mix the water with the pito yeast and add to the meat or fish. Add the chopped onions. Blend the tomatoes and chillies and add with the season all. Cook until the meat is tender. Serve hot with fufu.

# GROUNDNUT OR PEANUT BUTTER SOUP (NKATIE WONU)

*1 cup peanut butter (smooth) or groundnut paste*
*1 medium onion (chopped)*
*250 gms smoked fish (of your choice)*
*3 garden eggs (optional)*
*1 tin plum tomatoes (400 gms)*
*chillies to taste*
*500 gms mutton*
*1 Maggi cube*
*1 teaspoon fresh ground ginger*
*salt to taste*
*2.25 litres water*

*Serves 6*

Wash and cut the mutton into pieces, put into a saucepan with the chopped onions, salt, Maggi cube and a little water. Place on the fire. Wash and add the garden eggs and chillies and cook until tender. Remove from the saucepan. Mix the peanut butter or groundnut paste with the rest of the water and add to the soup. Blend the tomatoes and chillies and add to the soup. Add the ginger. Add the smoked fish. Reduce the heat and cook slowly for 30 mins. Remove the skin and seeds of the garden eggs and return to the soup. Serve hot with fufu, boiled yam, fried plantain or rice.

# PALMNUT GROUNDNUT SOUP (NKATE BE)

*1 small tin trofa or Ghanaian palmnut soup*
*1 kilo mutton or boiling chicken pieces*
*½ kilo smoked fish*
*1 tin plum tomatoes (400 gms)*
*100 gms peanut butter or groundnut paste*
*4 garden eggs*
*4 okras*
*1 large onion*
*1.5 litres water*
*1 teaspoon season all*
*chillies to taste*
*1 chicken stock cube or lamb stock cube*

*Serves 3*

Wash and cut up the mutton or chicken pieces and put into a saucepan with the chopped onions, season all and a very little water. Place on the stove. Blend the tomatoes and chillies and add to the pan. Now add the stock cube. Mix the peanut butter or groundnut paste with the palmnut soup and water. Add to the pan. If the fish is used, add at this stage. Season to taste. Cook for 1 hr 30 mins. Cook the garden eggs and okras separately and serve with the dish. Serve hot with fufu or rice.

# CORNDOUGH AND CHICKEN SOUP (FOTOLI)

*1 chicken (cut into pieces)*
*1 large onion*
*3 cups fermented corndough*
*chillies/salt to taste*
*1 tin plum tomatoes (400 gms)*
*1 pint palm oil*
*1 chicken stock cube*

*Serves 6*

Wash the chicken pieces and put into a saucepan. Add the chopped onions and palm oil and fry for 10 mins. Add enough water to cover the chicken. Add the stock cube. Blend the tomatoes with the chillies and add to the chicken. Mix a little corndough with water and add to the soup. Roll the rest of the corndough into small balls and add to the soup. Season to taste and cook until the chicken is tender. Serve hot.

# PALMNUT SOUP (NME WONU)

*1 large tin trofu or Ghanaian palmnut soup*
*750 gms mutton or boiling chicken pieces*
*1 tin plum tomatoes (400 gms)*
*1 Maggi cube or chicken stock cube*
*1 clove garlic*
*1 large onion*
*chillies (boiled and blended)*
*season all*
*1 teaspoon crushed fresh ginger*

*Serves 6*

Wash and cut the meat or boiling chicken pieces and put into a saucepan. Add the season all, chopped onions and crushed clove of garlic and put on the stove. Allow to cook in its own juices for 10 mins. Add the hot water to the trofu or Ghanaian palmnut soup and add to the contents in the saucepan. Blend the tomatoes and add to the soup. Add the blended pepper and ginger and leave to cook for 1 hr until the meat or chicken is tender. Add the Maggi cube or chicken stock cube and simmer gently until thick and the palm oil floats on the top. Serve with fufu rice, yams or boiled plantains.
Fresh fish or smoked fish can be used with mutton. If smoked fish is used add a little salt fish to the soup.

# Light Soup (Nkrakra)

1 boiling chicken (cut into pieces)
1 clove garlic
1 dessertspoon tomato puree
1 teaspoon ground fresh ginger
1 large onion
1 tin plum tomatoes (400 gms)
1 chicken stock cube, water
1 teaspoon fresh or dried basil leaves
chillies and salt to taste
2 large carrots

Serves 6

Wash the chicken pieces and put into a saucepan with half of the onion (chopped), crushed garlic, ginger, stock cube, basil and tomato puree. Cook for 20 mins. Blend the tomatoes with the other half of the onion and chillies and add to the chicken. Cover with enough water to fill the saucepan. Peel and chop the carrots and add to the soup. Cook for 1 hr 30 mins or until the chicken is tender. Season to taste. Serve hot with fufu, boiled yam or potatoes.
See Appendix for Fufu, Banku and Tuo recipes.

*Porridges*

# Corn Porridge (Akasa)

*1 cup fermented corndough*
*1 litre water*
*salt to taste*
*sugar to taste*
*milk (optional)*
*1 egg (optional)*

*Serves 6*

Mix the corndough with ½ litre of water and strain through a sieve into a saucepan. Boil the other ½ litre of water. Add to the mixture, and stir to avoid lumps. Cook and stir for 25 mins. Add sugar and milk. Add the beaten yolk of an egg when given to children. Can be served with roasted peanuts.

# Roasted Cornmeal Porridge (Ablemanu)

*1 cup roasted cornmeal*
*3 cups water*
*salt to taste*
*milk and sugar*

*Serves 3*

Mix the cornmeal with $1/_3$ of the water into a paste. Bring the rest of the water to the boil, then add to the paste. Stir to prevent lumps and add the salt. Cook on a low heat, stirring well until thick and smooth. Add the sugar and milk to taste. Serve hot.

# GRIT PORRIDGE (EKUEGBEN)

*1 cup grit (cornmeal)*
*sugar to taste*
*½ cup ground rice*
*milk*
*1 tablespoon margarine*
*3 cups water*

*Serves 4*

Mix the cornmeal, ground rice and a pint of water. Boil the rest of the water, add the mixture, and stir all the time. Cook on a low heat stirring to avoid lumps. Add the margarine. Serve hot with milk and sugar.
Can be flavoured with 2 tablespoons of peanut butter.

# Ripe Plantain and Corn Porridge (Olor)

*3 over-ripe plantain*
*salt and pepper to taste*
*1 cup fermented corndough*
*1 litre water*

*Serves 4*

Peel the plantain and put into a saucepan. Add 2 cups of water and salt. Boil until very soft and mash. Mix the corndough with water, strain and add the liquid to the mashed plantain. Add the pepper and salt to taste. Boil until the porridge is thick and free from lumps. Serve hot.

*Frying – Fried Foods*

# Lamb Stew (Tooloo Stew)

*1 kilo lamb (boneless and chopped)*
*1 dessertspoon tomato puree*
*cooking oil (of your choice)*
*1 teaspoon curry powder*
*1 large onion*
*½ teaspoon white pepper*
*1 tin plum tomatoes (240 gms)*
*chillies and salt to taste*
*1 Maggi cube*
*season all*

*Serves 6*

Season the lamb with season all, then fry in oil allowing to brown on both sides. Cover the frying pan and let the steam help to cook the lamb. Cook slowly for 20 mins, turning to prevent burning. Remove and make stew.

To make stew: Fry the chopped onions in oil. Add the blended tomatoes with chillies. Add the tomato puree. Fry until cooked. Add the Maggi cube, curry powder and white pepper. Season to taste. Serve with rice or yam.

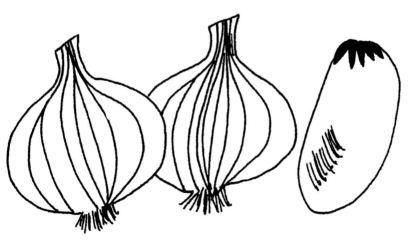

# Fried Fish (Kenan)

*fish (of your choice)*
*1 teaspoon ground ginger*
*6 snappers (medium)*
*salt and pepper to taste*
*1 cup cooking oil*
*2 small onions (ground)*
*vinegar*

*Serves 4*

Scale, clean and cut the fish into pieces. Marinade in the vinegar for 15 mins, then remove and dry. Season with salt and pepper and dry. Slit the fish on both sides and stuff with the ground onion, ginger and pepper. Fry in a shallow pan with enough hot oil to cover the bottom of the pan until brown on both sides. Serve with kenkey, gravy or rice.

# GRAVY FOR KENAN

*1 medium onion*
*1 teaspoon crushed fresh ginger*
*1 tin plum tomatoes (240 gms)*
*all purpose seasoning*
*1 clove garlic*
*½ cup cooking oil*
*½ teaspoon black pepper*
*1 teaspoon tomato puree*

*Serves 4*

Slice the onion and fry with the crushed garlic. Add the blended tomatoes with the tomato puree. Add the pepper. Season to taste. Spoon over the fish.

# PLANTAIN PANCAKES (TATALE)

*6 very ripe plantains*
*3 small onions*
*½ cup ground rice or semolina*
*1 teaspoon ground fresh ginger*
*1 cup cooking oil of your choice*
*½ cup self raising flour*
*2 eggs*
*season all to taste*

*Serves 4*

Peel and chop the onions and put into a food processor. Peel and cut up the plantain and add to the onions. Add the egg, ground rice or semolina with the flour, eggs and season all. Now blend until the mixture is smooth. Allow to stand for 30 mins. Fry in spoonfuls in a shallow pan with a little hot oil. Serve hot.

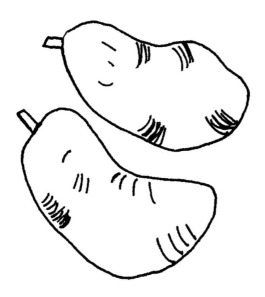

# POTATO OR YAM BALLS (YELE KAKRO)

*2 cups cooked mashed yam or potato*
*2 tablespoons margarine*
*½ cup milk*
*1 egg*
*salt and pepper to taste*

*Serves 2*

Mix the yam or potato with the pepper, salt, margarine, egg and milk together in a bowl. Form into balls and shallow fry. Serve hot with stew.

# Fried Plantain (Kelewele)

*2 ripe plantains*
*1 teaspoon ground ginger*
*1 teaspoon season all*
*1 small onion (ground)*
*2 cups cooking oil (of your choice)*

*Serves 2*

Wash and peel the plantains and cut up into small pieces. Rub with the season all, ground ginger and ground onion. Heat the oil until hot. Fry the plantain until golden brown. Drain on a kitchen towel to remove any excess fat. Serve as a dessert with peanuts.

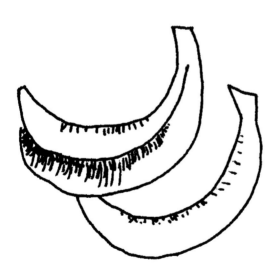

# FRIED YAM (YELE)
*(Recipe dedicated to Andy Kenworthy)*

*½ kilo yam*
*550 ml cooking oil*
*salt to taste*

*Serves 2*

Peel and cut the yam into pieces like thick chips. Towel dry the yam and season with salt. Dry fry the yam chips in hot oil until golden brown. Serve with pepper sauce or stew of your choice. Cocoyam, cassava and sweet potato can be fried in this method.

# Bean Cakes (Koosey)

*2 cups black-eyed beans*
*1 medium onion*
*1 egg beaten*
*2 cups cooking oil*
*salt and pepper to taste*
*½ cup water*

*Serves 4*

Soak the beans overnight, then remove the skin and eyes of the beans. Wash the beans thoroughly then put into a food processor and blend. Add the pepper and chopped onions and blend. Put the mixture into a bowl and mix with water. Beat to allow air in. Add the beaten egg and season to taste. Deep fry by dropping spoonfuls of the mixture into very hot oil. Fry until golden brown. Serve hot or cold.
Can be served in a buffet or as a dessert.

*Steamed Dishes*

# Steamed Cornmeal (Kpokpoi)
*A special dish for the Ga Festival*

*6 cups dry cornmeal*
*1 pint palm oil*
*6 okras (lady fingers)*
*4 tablespoons corndough*
*salt*

*Serves 8*

Sprinkle a little water over the cornmeal and leave it overnight. Rub through a sieve. Place a steamer over a saucepan of boiling water and seal the edges with a little cornmeal. Cover the bottom of the steamer with a little muslin, then put the sieved cornmeal into the steamer and let it cook over the steam for 30 mins. When cooked it will give out a yeasty aroma. Chop the okras and cook in a very little water until tender. Mash and add salt. When the Kpokpoi is taken out of the steamer, sprinkle with salted cold water. Use a wooden spoon to break up the lumps. Mix with the okras and stir. Add heated palm oil, until even. Serve with palm nut soup cooked only with fish.

# STEAMED BEANS (ALELEE OR MOIMOI)

*3 cups ground beans*
*2 teaspoons all purpose seasoning*
*½ pint palm oil or cooking oil*
*2 Maggi cubes*
*4 small onions aluminium foil for wrapping*
*1 cup powdered fish*
*water*
*chillies to taste*

*Serves 6*

Chop the onions and put into a blender with the ground beans. Mix with a little water. Pour a little boiling water into the dough and stir into a smooth paste. Add the all purpose seasoning, Maggi cubes, oil, fish and chillies. Divide into portions and wrap each in aluminium foil or put into foil pudding basins and cover. Put a steamer on the stove and arrange into the steamer. Steam for 1 hr 30 mins.

# Steamed Maize Meal (Aboloo)
## (Auntie Deidei's Special)

*4 cups maize meal*
*salt to taste*
*sugar to taste*
*1 cup self raising flour*
*2 teaspoons yeast*
*some water*
*aluminium foil*

*Serves 6*

Divide the maize meal into two halves. Then cook one half with the water and salt as for porridge for 10 mins. Leave to cool and then mix it with the raw maize meal. Mix the yeast with lukewarm water and add to the mixture. Then add the flour and sugar. Leave for a few hours. Put spoonfuls of the mixture into aluminium foil and parcel, then arrange them in the steamer. Cover and steam over boiling water for 10 mins or spread the parcels on a baking tray and bake in a moderate oven, gas mark 6 or 375°F, for 10 mins. Serve with stew or fried fish.

# Roasted Cornmeal Cakes (Kaakro)

*6 very ripe plantains*
*1 cup ground roasted cornmeal*
*4 small onions*
*1 teaspoon season all*
*2 cups cooking oil*

*Serves 4*

Peel and cut up the plantain and put into a food processor. Add the ground cornmeal with the chopped onions and 1 teaspoon of season all, and blend. Allow to stand for 30 mins. Deep fry in very hot oil in small balls or use a spoon to drop the mixture into the oil. Fry until golden brown. Drain and serve hot.

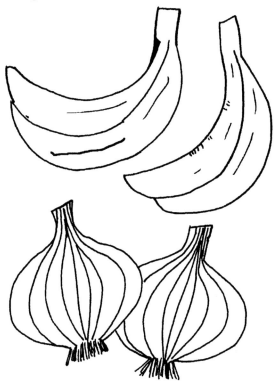

*Stewing*

# LAMB OR CHICKEN STEW

*1 kilo chopped lamb or 2 kilos chicken pieces*
*1 large onion*
*1 teaspoon mixed herbs*
*1 tin plum tomatoes (400 gms)*
*salt to taste*
*1 dessertspoon tomato puree*
*chilli powder to taste*
*1 chicken/lamb stock cube*
*cooking oil*
*1 clove garlic (crushed)*
*water*

*Serves 8*

Wash and season the chicken pieces or lamb with the crushed garlic, stock cube, a little salt and mixed herbs. Fry the lamb or chicken in hot oil until brown, then remove from the frying pan. Chop the onions and blend the plum tomatoes. Fry the onions and tomatoes. Add chilli to taste. Add the tomato puree and some water. Allow to simmer. Add the chicken or lamb to the stew and leave to cook until the lamb or chicken is tender. Stir occasionally to prevent burning. Serve with rice, yam or potatoes.

# LIVER STEW

*½ kilo lamb's liver*
*150 ml cooking oil*
*½ teaspoon all purpose seasoning*
*1 tin plum tomatoes (400 gms)*
*chilli powder to taste*
*1 Maggi cube*
*1 large onion*
*½ teaspoon mixed spice or nutmeg*

*Serves 6*

Use the same method as for lamb or chicken stew but add mixed spice or nutmeg. Serve with rice or aboloo.
N.B. Do not overcook the liver.

# Jollof Rice with Chicken or Lamb

*1 kilo lamb (chopped)*
*cooking oil*
*1½ kilos chicken pieces*
*500 gms rice*
*1 tin plum tomatoes (400 gms)*
*1 teaspoon mixed herbs*
*1 large onion*
*½ teaspoon nutmeg*

*1 dessertspoon tomato puree*
*salt*
*1 Maggi cube*
*½ teaspoon white pepper*
*1 clove crushed garlic*
*250 gms mixed vegetables*
*1.5 litres water*

*Serves 6*

Wash and season the chicken or lamb with salt, garlic and mixed herbs. Fry in hot oil, then put into a saucepan with 2 cups of water and place on the fire. Chop the onions and blend the tomatoes. Fry and add to the saucepan. Add the Maggi cube, water, nutmeg, white pepper and tomato puree. Wash the rice and add when the lamb/chicken is almost tender. Boil the rice with the mixed vegetables for 10 mins then reduce the heat and simmer until cooked. Stir frequently to avoid burning and keep the lid on all the time. Serve hot with mixed salad.

# FISH STEW

*1 kilo fresh fish*
*½ teaspoon thyme*
*1 tin plum tomatoes (400 gms)*
*Salt and chilli to taste*
*1 large onion*
*cooking oil*
*1 clove garlic*
*850 ml water*
*1 teaspoon ground coriander*
*½ teaspoon white pepper*
*vinegar*

*Serves 6*

Scale and wash the fish and cut into pieces. Wash in vinegar. Season the fish with garlic and salt and fry in hot oil until brown on both sides. Slice the onions and fry. Blend the tomatoes and add to the onions with the chillies. Add the water and allow to simmer for 15 mins. Add the fish, thyme, coriander, white pepper and salt. Cover and simmer for 20 mins, stirring gently. Serve with rice, yam, aboloo or potatoes.

# PALM OIL STEW

*1 kilo smoked fish*
*1 tablespoon flour*
*1 tin plum tomatoes (400 gms)*
*1 teaspoon season all*
*1 large onion*
*chilli powder to taste*
*1 teaspoon crushed fresh ginger*
*200 ml palm oil*
*850 ml water*
*50 gms salt fish*
*1 shrimp stock cube*

*Serves 6*

Slice the onions, then blend the tomatoes with the chilli. Fry the onions with the palm oil in a saucepan. Add the salt fish, tomatoes, chillies and ginger and fry for a few minutes. Add the water and allow to simmer for 10 mins. Then add the shrimp stock cube. Add the smoked fish, then mix the flour with a little cold water to a smooth paste and add. Cover and simmer for 25 mins, stirring to prevent burning. Serve with vegetables.

# AGUSI STEW

*200 gms agusi*
*1 tin plum tomatoes (240 gms)*
*1 kilo mutton or smoked fish or ½ kilo of each*
*salt and chilli to taste*
*300 ml palm oil or cooking oil*
*1 large onion*
*1 Maggi cube*
*water*

*Serves 6*

Cut the mutton into pieces and prepare as for stew. Put into a saucepan. Add the salt and water and cook until tender. Slice the onions. Blend the tomatoes with the chilli and agusi and fry in oil, then add to the saucepan. Add the smoked fish and allow to simmer for a while. Add the Maggi cube. Simmer until it is well stewed. Serve with rice or vegetables.

# Nkotomire Stew
# (Cocoyam/Darshin Leaf)

*½ kilo cocoyam/darshin leaves*
*150 ml palm oil*
*1 large onion*
*salt and chilli to taste*
*1 tin plum tomatoes (240 gms)*
*300 ml water*
*½ kilo smoked fish*
*1 vegetable stock cube*
*50 gms salt fish*

*Serves 6*

Wash and pick the cocoyam leaves well and then shred. Slice the onions. Blend the tomatoes with the chilli, then fry in the palm oil and add the salt fish. Add the water. Wash and break up the smoked fish into pieces and add to the stew. Add the shredded cocoyam leaves to the stew with the stock cube and season to taste (you can add 1 cup chopped peanuts at this stage). Let it simmer for 5 mins. Serve with boiled green plantains, yam or potatoes.

# Palaver Sauce (Spinach Stew)

*½ kilo fresh or frozen spinach*
*salt and chilli to taste*
*1 dessertspoon dried shrimp powder*
*1 tin plum tomatoes (400 gms)*
*½ kilo smoked fish*
*425 ml palm oil*
*1 large onion water*
*100 gms ground agusi*
*½ kilo mutton*
*1 teaspoon fresh ground ginger*
*1 clove crushed garlic*
*1 stock cube*

*Serves 6*

Wash and cut the mutton into pieces and season with the garlic, salt and ginger. Cook until tender. Slice the onions. Blend the tomatoes with the chilli, then fry in oil and add to the mutton. Add the ground agusi with a little water and add to the stew as well as the dried shrimp powder. Add the stock cube. Add the smoked fish and let it simmer for a while. Pick the veins off the leaves and wash well, then shred and add to the stew or add the frozen spinach. Simmer for 30 mins, stirring occasionally. Serve hot with rice, plantains or yam.

# Garden Egg or Aubergine Stew

*20 garden eggs or 3 large Aubergines*
*300 ml palm oil or cooking oil*
*1 tin plum tomatoes (400 gms)*
*chilli powder to taste*
*salt*
*½ kilo smoked fish*
*½ kilo stewing lamb*
*1 vegetable stock cube*
*1 teaspoon season all*

*Serves 8*

Cut up the stewing lamb and season with the season all and boil until tender, then add the fish. Chop the onions and fry in hot palm oil or cooking oil in a saucepan. Add the blended tomatoes, the chilli and vegetable stock cube and cook for 10 mins. Chop the garden eggs or peel and chop the aubergines. Add the meat, fish and stock and cook until the garden eggs are done, then gently cook until the oil comes to the top. Season with salt and serve with boiled rice, yam, plantain or banku.

# Okro Stew (Okra)

Use the same recipe as for Garden Egg Stew but reduce the garden eggs to 10 and the aubergines to 2. Use ½ kilo of okras (chopped), then add the okras at the same time as the garden eggs and aubergines.

*Roasts*

# Roast Pork (Domedo)

*2 kilos pork (boneless)*
*chilli pepper to taste*
*1 large onion*
*1 tablespoon fresh ground ginger*
*1 teaspoon jerk seasoning*
*3 fresh tomatoes*

*Serves 10*

Clean and dry the pork. Grate the onion and ginger. Rub the salt, chilli, onion, ginger and jerk seasoning into the pork. Place the pork into a roasting pan, and roast in a slow oven Gas Mark 4 or 350°F for 2 hrs 30 mins. When cooked pour the stock from the pork into a saucepan and make an accompaniment sauce to go with it. Chop the tomatoes and add to the stock. Cook for 10 mins. Serve with the sauce and hot kenkey.

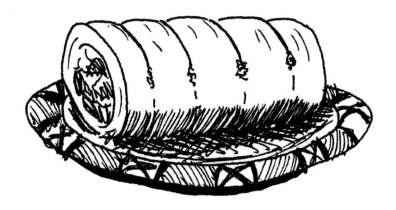

# Pot Roast Beef or Lamb

*1 kilo boneless rolled beef/lamb*
*salt and pepper to taste*
*600 gms margarine*
*1 medium onion*
*1 gill stock or water*
*1 teaspoon ground aniseed*
*2 tomatoes*

*Serves 6*

Wash and season the beef or lamb with salt and pepper and ground aniseed. Melt the margarine in a pot with a fitted lid. Pot roast the beef or lamb until thoroughly brown, then cover the pot and reduce the heat. Allow to cook slowly, turning frequently, until the beef is tender, then remove. Slice the onions and fry with the chopped tomatoes. Add the white pepper to the fat used to roast the beef or lamb. Add the stock and season to taste. Allow to simmer for 10 mins. Skim and place the beef on a serving dish and pour round the beef or lamb. Garnish with slices of fresh tomatoes and green pepper.

# Roast Chicken

*1½ kilo chicken*

*Serves 4*

Use the same method for roast beef, but season the chicken with seasoning of your own choice. Stuffing should be cooked separately. Chicken can be pot roasted or roasted in the oven for 1 hr 30 mins.

*Cakes*

# Marian's Fruit Cake
## For Weddings, Birthdays or Christmas

170 gms currants
½ grated lemon rind
115 gms sultanas
½ grated orange rind
55 gms raisins
1 tablespoon white rum or local gin
55 gms glace cherries
115 gms plain flour
55 gms mixed peel

½ teaspoon nutmeg
30 gms peanut butter
½ teaspoon mixed spice
100 gms soft margarine
½ teaspoon cinnamon
100 gms soft brown sugar
2 eggs
½ tablespoon black treacle
1 teaspoon vanilla essence

Weigh the dried fruit, cherries and peanuts into a bowl. Add the lemon rind, orange rind, peanut butter, black treacle and rum or local gin and soak for a couple of days. Cream the margarine and sugar. Add the eggs, flour, nutmeg, mixed spice, cinnamon and vanilla essence. Add to the bowl with the fruits and mix. Leave to stand for 1 hr. Grease and line a 6 inch round cake tin or a 5 inch square tin. Put the mixture into the tin and bake at Gas Mark 1 or 290°F for 1 hr 30 mins to 2 hrs. Stick a skewer into the cake. If it comes out clean the cake is cooked. Leave to cool in the tin before turning out.

# MARIAN'S SPECIAL CAKE

*200 gms margarine*
*4 eggs*
*30 gms butter*
*a little lemon juice*
*170 gms caster sugar*
*½ teaspoon nutmeg*
*200 gms self raising flour*
*½ teaspoon vanilla essence*
*30 gms wholemeal self raising flour*
*½ teaspoon almond essence*

Cream the margarine, butter and sugar together, then add the eggs and lemon juice. Add the self raising and wholemeal flour to the mixture, then add the flavourings and nutmeg. Leave to stand for 30 mins. Grease and line an 8 inch round tin and bake in a moderate oven Gas Mark 4 or 160°F for 1 hr. Test with a skewer, if it comes out clean the cake is cooked. Take out of the oven and leave in the tin to cool before turning out.

# MARIAN'S GARI CAKE

*Same ingredients as for Marian's Special Cake.*

After adding the flour, add 1 tablespoon of gari with a little milk to get a dropping consistency.

# MARIAN'S SEMOLINA CAKE

*Same ingredients as for Marian's Special Cake*

After adding the flour add 1 tablespoon of semolina, ½ teaspoon of mixed spice and a little milk then bake.


# MARIAN'S GROUND RICE CAKE

*Same ingredients as for Marian's Special Cake*

After adding the flour add 1 tablespoon of ground rice, ½ teaspoon of coconut essence and a little milk then follow through.

# Yellow Corn Cake (Eburow Cake)

*225 gms margarine*
*450 gms mixed dried fruits*
*170 gms caster sugar*
*½ gill brandy*
*4 eggs*
*½ tablespoon chopped peanuts*
*115 gms plain flour*
*½ teaspoon mixed spices*
*115 gms yellow cornmeal*

Cream the margarine and sugar until fluffy. Add the eggs one at a time. Fold in the flour and mixed spice, then add the peanuts and mixed fruit. Add the brandy and mix to a dropping consistency. You can add a little milk if required. Leave to stand for 30 mins. Grease and line a 9 inch cake tin. Put the cake mixture into the tin and top with peanuts. Then bake in a moderate oven for 3 hrs, or until cooked. Take out of the oven and leave to cool before turning out.

# Plantain Cake (Ablongo)

*8 soft ripe plantains*
*salt and white pepper to taste*
*1 medium onion*
*500 ml palm oil or cooking oil*
*1 teaspoon fresh ground ginger*
*½ cup water*
*1 cup ground rice or semolina*
*1 egg*

*Serves 6*

Wash and peel the plantains, chop and put into a food processor.
Add the egg, chopped onions, ginger, ground rice or semolina, salt,
pepper and water. Mix until smooth then add the palm oil. You can
use ordinary cooking oil. Grease a bread loaf tin with palm oil or
cooking oil and fill with the mixture. Bake in a moderate oven for
1 hr 30 mins. May be served hot or cold.

# CASSAVA CAKE (KOKONTE D'ABAM)

*450 gms cassava flour*
*125 gms melted margarine*
*1 cup milk*
*1 teaspoon nutmeg*
*200 gms grated coconut or ½ packet (125 gms) creamed coconut*
*2 teaspoons cinnamon*
*a pinch of salt*
*100 gms sugar*
*100 gms mixed fruit*
*1 egg*
*1 teaspoon vanilla essence*
*4 tablespoons baking powder*

*Serves 6*

This is a one stage mixture. Put all ingredients into a bowl or food processor and mix to a dropping consistency. Grease and line a 9 inch cake tin and put mixture into the tin. Bake in a moderate oven for 30 mins. When cooked, leave in the tin to cool.

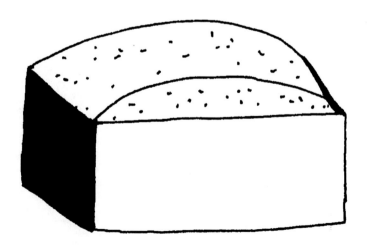

*Biscuits*

# Peanut or Groundnut Biscuits

*½ cup margarine*
*a pinch of salt*
*1/3 cup sugar*
*1 cup chopped peanuts or groundnuts*
*1½ cups self raising flour*
*1 grated rind of lemon*
*1 egg*
*1 dessertspoon peanut butter or groundnut paste*
*a few drops vanilla essence*

Cream the margarine and sugar, add the egg, vanilla, grated rind of lemon and peanut butter/groundnut paste. Add the flour, pinch of salt and peanuts/groundnuts. Drop from a tablespoon onto a greased baking sheet and flatten with a fork. Bake in a moderate hot oven for 10–15 mins.

# GARI BISCUITS

*125 gms fine gari*
*1 teaspoon lemon juice*
*125 gms self raising flour*
*½ teaspoon grated lemon rind*
*125 gms margarine*
*½ beaten egg*
*120 gms sugar*

This is a one stage mix. Put all the ingredients into a food processor or a bowl and mix until it forms a dough. Roll out the mixture on a floured surface to ⅛ inch thick and use different shapes of biscuit cutters to cut out biscuits. Prick the biscuits with a fork and place on a greased baking tray. Bake in a moderate oven for 15 mins. Cool on a wire rack and store in a biscuit tin.

# Coconut Biscuits

*125 gms margarine*
*1 tablespoon desiccated coconut*
*125 gms caster sugar*
*pinch of salt*
*175 gms self raising flour*
*1 egg*
*1 teaspoon lemon juice*

Cream the margarine and sugar. Add the flour and salt. Add the beaten egg and coconut and work into a dough. Roll out to $\frac{1}{8}$ inch thick and cut out with biscuit cutters. Prick the biscuits. Place on greased baking trays and bake in a moderate oven for 15 mins. Cool and store in a biscuit tin.

*Bread*

# PALM WINE BREAD

*1.5 kilos plain flour*
*a pinch of salt*
*350 ml palm wine (or white wine)*
*250 gms margarine*
*300 ml lukewarm water*
*2 eggs*
*1 teaspoon cinnamon*

Mix the palm wine or white wine with water, sugar, salt, margarine and eggs, then add the flour and cinnamon. Mix into a soft dough and knead well. Put into a basin, cover and put into a warm place (perhaps under a grill) to rise. Turn onto a lightly floured board and knead into small loaves. Put into greased bread tins. Allow to rise again. Bake in a hot oven for 50 mins.

# CORNMEAL ROLLS

*3 cups cornmeal*
*1 egg*
*1½ cups boiling water*
*1/3 cup margarine*
*1½ tablespoons compressed yeast*
*3/4 cup powdered skimmed milk*
*1/3 cup soft brown sugar*
*5 cups plain flour*
*a pinch of salt*
*1 teaspoon nutmeg*

Put the margarine, sugar, nutmeg and cornmeal into a bowl or food processor. Mix with boiling water. When lukewarm add the egg, yeast, skimmed milk and half of the flour. Beat until smooth, then add the rest of the flour and knead into a dough. Wrap in greaseproof paper. Place in a bowl and cover with a towel. Allow to rise in a warm place for 1 hr. Knead into small rolls about 70 gms in weight. Place on greased trays and cover. Allow to rise again for 1 hr. Then bake in a moderate oven, Gas Mark 6 or 375°F for 30 mins.

*Party Dishes*

# WAAKYE (RICE AND BEANS)
*(pronounced Waachay)*

1 cup long grain rice
1/4 chopped onion
1 cup dried black-eyed beans or kidney beans
1 teaspoon creamed coconut
½ teaspoon salt
1 Maggi cube
½ teaspoon bicarbonate of soda
1 teaspoon oregano or thyme or mixed herbs or tarragon leaves

Soak the black-eyed beans in water overnight. Wash the black-eyed beans and put into a saucepan then cover with 3 cups of water. Cook the beans for 15 mins then add the salt, oregano or thyme or mixed herbs or tarragon leaves and bicarbonate of soda. Cook for another 30 mins then wash the rice and add to the beans. Add the Maggi cube, chopped onions and creamed coconut. Add enough water to bring the rice and beans to the boil, then lower the heat and steam cook, stirring occasionally. When cooked, both the rice and beans will be soft to the touch. Serve with shitor (pepper sauce) or chicken stew or fish stew or meat stew with fried plantains and a mixed salad or coleslaw.

# Azikoliko (Fried Yams or Sweet Potato with Eggs)

*6 slices cooked yam or sweet potato*
*1/4 cup cooking oil*
*1 teaspoon season all*
*2 eggs (beaten)*
*2 chillies*
*1 medium sized onion*

Blend the onions, chillies and season all together and add the beaten eggs. Cut the cooked yam or sweet potato into triangles or rounds and dip into the egg mixture. Heat up the cooking oil in a frying pan and fry both sides until golden brown. Drain on kitchen paper and serve hot.

P.S. You may use slices of kenkey or potatoes or any starchy foods.

# DZEMKPLE (ROAST CORNMEAL TURN)
*(Pronounced Jempelay)*

*1½ cups roasted cornmeal*
*½ cup palm oil or cooking oil*
*1 medium size onion*
*2 cups water*
*4 chillies*
*1 teaspoon salt*
*a little salt fish*
*1 Maggi cube*
*smoked fish of your choice (if desired)*

*Serves 4*

Blend the onion, chillies, salt and Maggi cube together. Heat the palm oil or cooking oil in a saucepan and add the blended ingredients and salt fish to it. Sauté for 5 mins. Wash the smoked fish, remove the bones and flake. Add to the mixture. Add water and bring to the boil. Sprinkle the cornmeal on to the water, continuously stirring to prevent lumps. Add the rest of the cornmeal slowly, stirring the mixture, turning it over and over with a wooden spoon until it is firm to the touch. Dish it out in spoonfuls or in rounds. Serve hot with barbecued chicken.

# VARIATION 1 (APELEGEE)

Use 2½ cups cooked palmnut soup instead of palm oil or cooking oil and water. Add the blended ingredients and stir in the cornmeal. Serve with crabs.

# VARIATION 2

Add 1 cup of cooked red beans or broad beans when adding water
and bringing to the boil.

*Sauces*

# SHITOR (PEPPER SAUCE)

*2 large onions*
*4 tablespoons ground shrimps*
*2 cloves garlic (crushed)*
*1 teaspoon tomato paste*
*1 tablespoon fresh ground ginger*
*1 teaspoon ground coriander*
*1 dessertspoon ground chillies*
*1 teaspoon rosemary*
*2 Maggi cubes*
*½ cup cooking oil*
*salt and pepper to taste*

Chop the onions finely, then fry in a saucepan with the crushed garlic and ground ginger until the onions are soft. Add the ground dried shrimps, ground chillies, tomato paste, ground coriander and rosemary. Add the Maggi cubes until it is all cooked and blended and the oil separates from the shitor. Season to taste. Cool and store in jam jars. Serve with rice and beans, kenkey and fish or as a condiment with foods of your choice. This goes well with fried yam.

# Marian's Mild Pepper Sauce

*2 large onions (chopped)*
*75 ml cooking oil*
*6 fresh tomatoes (1 tin plum tomatoes 240 gms)*
*½ teaspoon chilli powder*
*1 green sweet pepper (chopped)*
*75 ml tarragon vinegar*
*1 red sweet pepper (chopped)*
*1 teaspoon mixed spice*
*1 clove garlic (crushed)*
*salt and pepper to taste*

Fry the chopped onions and crushed garlic in oil for 2 mins, then add the vinegar. Chop the tomatoes and add. Fry for 2 mins. Add the chopped peppers, chilli powder and mixed spice. Fry until the tomatoes are cooked and well blended. Add salt and pepper to taste. Store in heated jam jars. Serve with pasta, rice, cold meats or foods of your choice.

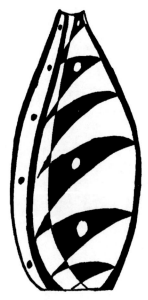

*Appendix*

# Banku (Turned Cornmeal)

*1 cup fermented corn dough*
*1½ cups water*
*1/4 teaspoon salt*

*Serves 2*

Mix the corndough with water in a saucepan with a long handle, then add the salt. Put on medium heat on the cooker. Stir with a wooden spoon. Keep turning to avoid lumps until you hear a whistling sound and the mixture is firm. If the banku is too firm add a little water and stir well. Wet a soup bowl with water, and put the banku into it and turn it over into a dish. Serve with soup of your choice.

# FUFU (POTATO, PLANTAIN OR COCOYAM)

*1 cup instant mashed potato*
*½ cup farina (potato starch)*
*1½ cups water*

*Serves 2*

Use the same steps as the banku recipe. Plantain and cocoyam fufu come in packets and are sold in Ethnic food shops. Follow the instructions on the packet.

# OMOR TUO (RICEBALLS)

*1 cup rice*
*2 cups water*
*a pinch of taste*
*1 teaspoon margarine*

*Serves 2*

Wash the rice and put into a saucepan with a long handle, then add the salt and margarine and cover with a tight lid. Cook the rice over a medium heat and let it boil for 10 mins. Test the rice with your fingers and if too hard add another half cup of water to cook it until it is very soft and mashes easily. Use a wooden spoon to turn the rice until it forms one large lump. Use a wet ladle spoon to dish the rice out into balls. Serve with a soup of your choice.
Goes well with palmnut soup or groundnut (peanut butter) soup.

# Conclusion

I hope you have enjoyed the taste of heaven which is reflected in this gift of hospitality.

It is good to meet up with friends and family to share fellowship with food, but it is most important to have eternal food, the bread of life, to hunger and thirst for righteousness.

My secret recipe (costs nothing).

Food tastes better when glaced with a bit of gospel and mixed with the love of God. I invite you to consider my secret recipe and invite Jesus into your life, to join him in this Taste of Hospitality and his sweetness will be the dessert of your meal.

God Bless
Marian

To every believer – The digestive of our meal is:

Jesus you are the centre of our joy. All that is good and perfect comes from you. You are the source of our contentment and hope for all we do.

ISBN 155395218-9